THE ART AND CRAFT OF SAND CASTING

THE ART

SAND

with 54 photographs by the autho...

AND CRAFT OF

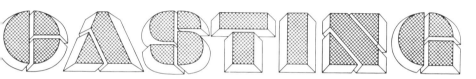

by Paul Villiard

FUNK & WAGNALLS

New York

DESIGNED BY LORETTA LI

Manufactured in the United States of America

Library of Congress Cataloging in Publication Data

Villiard, Paul.
    The art and craft of sand casting.

    1. Sand casting. I. Title.
TT295.V54 1975   731.4′52   74–28252
ISBN 0–308–10160–X

1 2 3 4 5 6 7 8 9 10

FOR ALINE STEYER
for her valuable assistance in preparing this volume

OTHER BOOKS BY PAUL VILLIARD:

Exotic Fish as Pets
A First Book of Ceramics
A First Book of Jewelrymaking
A First Book of Leatherworking
A Manual of Veneering
Moths and How to Rear Them
The Practical Candymaking Cookbook
Raising Small Animals for Fun and Profit
Reptiles as Pets
Shells: Home in the Sea
Through the Seasons with a Camera
Wild Mammals as Pets

CONTENTS

PART

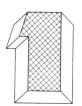

An
INTRODUCTION
to the
ART
of
SAND CASTING

ince prehistoric times man has endeavored to express himself in various ways. These methods of expression, or, to be more explicit, the art forms used have become more and more complex as our technology has advanced, until some of the media used require a mechanical knowledge far beyond the average artist or craftsman. An example of this use of industrial methods and equipment as a form of art expression is in the objects made of welded steel, brass, and other metals. Both welding and cutting techniques are employed, as well as the even more difficult techniques of cutting with an oxyacetylene torch.

In the past decade, however, there seems to be a trend toward the simplification of art expression, and a return to the use of more simple materials. One of these simplified forms is sand casting. When I mention sand casting to various people, the vast majority of them think at once of casting metal into forms made in sand. This is not really sand casting. It is casting in sand, and there is a difference. Casting in sand is the method used in foundries to make the various machine components and rough castings from which different items are finished.

Sand casting is an art form. A form of expression that is simple and effective in itself. It is the casting of plaster or cement into molds made in sand, with the deliberate intention of having the casting itself pick up a layer of sand on the surface. Thus, in sand casting, one achieves a three-dimensional object, which affords a contrast of light and shadow when viewed from different angles, and also a surface texture from the roughness of the coating of sand adhering to the surface.

WHAT TO MAKE

Practically anything may be used as an impression maker. Ordinary kitchen utensils, children's toys, objects around the house, pebbles, seashells, bits of minerals and rocks, spools, you name it, and it will have some application somewhere, in some kind of sand casting.

The objects made by this process are used in various manners. Wall plaques are perhaps the most popular, but there is no reason why other things of more useful purpose are not possible. By the use of weatherproof and waterproof casting materials, such things as sundials, for example, are not only possible, but ornamental and decorative as well.

Tiles can be made by the process, which can be used in bathrooms, or, in a larger form, to cover the foundations of your home. Certainly an improvement over the rather unsightly concrete block or poured foundation.

The design and diversity of tiles is limited only by your own imagination, and, by making a sturdy form in which to make the impressions in the sand, you can make as many as you like all the same size, shape, and design.

Naturally, if tiles were made for a bathroom wall, they would be used in that part of the room not subjected to constant touch and wear. The rough, sandy surface would make them rather uncomfortable in a situation like that. However, as a decorative band, border, or panel they would be extremely effective, and, if made from waterproof materials, should last as long as the bathroom itself.

Naturally, too, sand castings are somewhat crude by nature. They do not lend themselves very well to infinitely fine detail, but rather demand bolder design and configuration.

One of the appealing facets of this art form is the extreme simplicity of performance. Anybody can do it. Anybody can make objects which have that professional art look, since only a few things are necessary to achieve success in the work—the proper mixing of the plaster, the proper pouring into the mold, and the proper preparation of the mold itself.

MOLDS AND SLIP CASTING

To begin, think what it is exactly that you would like to make an impression of. Molds can be made anywhere there is sand. Many beautiful castings are made directly on beaches, and it is not at all unusual to see a person or a group of persons busily engaged in pouring plaster into hollowed-out cavities in the beach, adorning their work with shells and other items picked up from that same beach and incorporated into the mold.

However, if you feel unable to create your own designs do not hesitate to use prefabricated models. Throughout the country ceramics houses have sprung up, dealing in slipcast products. Slip casting is a form of ceramics designed to open that craft to those unable to create original items. The ceramics pieces are cast in plaster of paris molds, using clay that has been liquified into slip by the addition of water and chemicals that keep the clay in liquid suspension. The result is a perfect impression of whatever shape was in the mold—even to scratches and chips carelessly or accidently occurring.

We can easily borrow from this craft to make sand casting models. The ceramics places sell "greenware" literally in hundreds of different sizes and shapes. Greenware is raw, unfired ceramics, and, as such, is fragile in the extreme. If you do not have a kiln in which to fire the pieces, the stores selling them usually do, and, for a moderate fee will fire them for you. Once fired, the ceramics is known as bisque or biscuit ware, and it is then hard and permanent. The next step in making ceramics is to permanent. The next step in making ceramics is to glaze the ware, but this step need not be taken when using the ceramics as molds for sand casting. What you may do, however, is epoxy one or two short lengths of dowel to the backs of the ceramics pieces, to enable you to remove them from the sand casting box once the impression has been made.

When using ceramics greenware as models for casting, the cleaning up of the unfired clay piece need not be nearly as perfect as if the piece were going to be used as ceramics. The mold lines of the clay should be sanded away, any gross scratches or indents should be smoothed away, and that is about all you need to do with it. When the piece is placed into the sand, small blemishes will not show, or, if they do show in the sand, a slight pat or rub with a fingertip will erase them sufficiently to eliminate them from the cast surface.

MAKING A CASTING BOX

At home, sand casting can be done in any kind of container that will hold the sand.

The container can be made if you do not have one

Spraying the surface with enamel will help make cleaner impressions if you are making many from the same piece of bisque ware.

sufficiently large and strong enough to hold the molds you wish to cast. Lengths of common 2″ x 8″ building lumber probably make the best frame members for a casting box. These may be cut to any convenient length and nailed together to form a square or a rectangle. The bottom can be made of $\frac{1}{2}$″ or $\frac{3}{4}$″ plywood, cut to the overall size of the frame and securely nailed to one side of the 2 x 8s. The box need not be painted or otherwise treated, and it will last for years of casting. Two or more such boxes can be made if you intend doing much casting, and, if you wish to make a large series of things, as, for instance, enough tiles to cover your house foundation, then you could make smaller boxes out of thinner boards, the dimensions being just a little larger than the individual tiles, and a dozen or so of these can be put together. This way, you can run a kind of production line, saving much time and labor. The mold is pressed into the entire line of boxes, the plaster dribbled into one after the other, and the molds filled the same way. If you have an assistant, one can go down the line dribbling the first coat and the other can follow behind filling the mold. In this way the dribbled coating will not dry out so much as to cause separation of layers.

When making larger casting boxes, you should use either coated or galvanized nails, since the weight of the sand is such as to cause the bottom to pull loose if the box is moved about very much. A couple of handles fastened to opposite sides of large boxes will facilitate moving it about after it has been filled with sand. A box 20″ square or larger may require two people to move it, because of the weight involved.

The table upon which you work must be sturdy, and well braced to the floor, since considerable pressure can be exerted in pressing the mold into the sand, and a thin or wobbly work surface may well bow to the point of collapse if it is not sufficiently braced. A couple of heavy planks across two sawhorses make a good working support for a large sand casting box, and this has the added advantage of being easily disassembled when you have finished casting for the time being.

If you live in such a location as to make it difficult or impossible to construct your casting boxes out of lumber, then an excellent substitute, albeit a bit more expensive, is a mortar pan, sold in building supply houses. These are about 8″ deep, and one size, at least, is 22″ x 30″ in area, which is large enough for most sand casting. The mortar pans are made of sheet steel and will last for a lifetime of work. The cost can be considered an expenditure for a tool to practice your hobby, and, after several casts have been made, can be amortized among the finished pieces. In other words, if the pan cost you ten dollars, and you made twenty castings, then to the cost of the sand and plaster you would add fifty cents for the pan. This way it does not seem to be such an investment if it is necessary to purchase the tool.

Wooden crates may also be brought into use as sand casting boxes. Many of them are so deep as to require an enormous quantity of sand to fill them. If this is the case, they can be cut down, removing the bottom, cutting the sides to a more reasonable height, then renailing the bottom in place. Sometimes you can even make two casting boxes out of one crate, by sawing the crate in half horizontally, then putting a new bottom on the top half, leaving the old bottom in place on the original bottom half of the crate.

You do not even have to be careful that all seams are closed completely, as many crates have narrow spaces between the slats from which they are fashioned. The boxes can be lined with plastic sheeting found in lumber yards and building supply houses all over the country. The plastic can be fitted to the inside, folding the corners rather than cutting them, and the edges brought up over the top edges of the box and tacked in place. Or, failing to obtain plastic, cheap oilcloth from a dime store will serve just as well. Even aluminum foil could be used in a pinch, bearing in mind that this latter material will be subject to more damage during the passage of time than the plastic or oilcloth. Also, you are limited by the width of the rolls of aluminum sheeting while plastic and oilcloth can be obtained several feet in width.

Lining the sand casting boxes, even those you make out of heavy material, also adds the bonus of helping to keep the sand damp by forming an evaporation barrier inside the box. If, then, you make a cover for the box, you will find that once dampened the sand will retain enough moisture for casting for several days at a time, obviating the necessity of going to the trouble of wetting it down each time it is used.

TOOLS OF THE TRADE

Tools that are useful in sand casting are a child's set of toy garden tools. A small, short-handled rake, a toy hoe, a trowel, and perhaps a cultivator are all very useful in preparing sand for impressions. The rake is especially handy to level the surface of the sand in the box. Trowel and hoe may be used for scooping out the cavity to receive the mold when the latter is so deep as to necessitate the removal of sand before making the impression. The cultivator is very useful for raking local areas without disturbing the rest of the sand. A watering can of the sprinkler type is almost a must for use in dampening the sand as it dries out. A spout type of can is not as good, since the flow of water from the spout is strong enough to wash away sand in large quantities while the more gentle action of the type of can with a sprinkler nozzle does not do this.

A basin in which to mix the plaster must be used, and this should preferably be of plastic. A plastic wash basin is ideal. While the container can be of any material from an empty tin can on up, the plastic basin has many advantages. It is unbreakable, to begin with, and lightweight so it does not add materially to your burden when holding it filled with mixed plaster. If any plaster hardens in a plastic vessel, it is an easy matter to bend the vessel and snap loose the deposit of set-up plaster. In a metal or glass container you must chip and scrape away any plaster permitted to harden, which can become difficult to do.

If you are using picture wire for hangers, then you must, of course, have a pair of wire cutters. Any hardware store will sell these.

The sand used can be of many kinds. That found on the beach can be brought home in a sack or two. Sand found in building supply houses and lumber yards will serve admirably. The coarser sand used in the bottoms of aquariums, and purchased by the pound in pet stores is perfectly usable. As a matter of fact, pet stores sell coarse sand, or fine gravel in different colors, which can be used to advantage in many ways.

Areas in the sand casting box may be scooped out and filled with one color or another of this aquarium gravel, then the mold impression made in that, to pick up the color as an accented area, or to have the entire cast covered with the color. Colorwheel projects are made in this fashion, making good accent pieces for wall decoration.

PREPARING THE SAND TO
RECEIVE AN IMPRESSION

Sand casting cannot be easily performed unless the sand is damp to the point of adherence. It should not be wet, but rather damp enough to stand firm when a handful is squeezed together, yet it must be loose enough to receive the impression of the molds. A little experience will tell you the proper amount of moisture to add to the materials.

When fancy sands, like those from the pet stores mentioned earlier are used, you may have to play around quite a bit with moistening in order to arrive at the correct slump point, since some of these sands are colored by virtue of being coated with a plastic in liquid form, and do not retain the water when wetted down. Some of the very coarse grains also may be difficult to moisten, and these must be used as thin layers over regular dampened sand in order to achieve the desired effect.

Also, when using colored sands on top of the regular sand, the impression should be first made in the regular sand, then the colored sand sprinkled in place to cover the surface, then the impression remade on top of the colored material. Care must be taken not to push the colored sand so deeply into the base sand as to lose the effect, the casting picking up a mixture of both instead of just the color. Also care must be taken not to push aside the colored sand on corners and edges of the mold, to expose the base material.

The molds should be pushed down into the dampened sand in a straight and vertical direction. Do not rock the mold into place, since this will distort the cavity. If the mold is a deep one, you might be unable to push in the model to the proper depth without displacing some of the sand.

Also, many times, especially if you are casting in fine sand, you will have difficulty in pressing the mold in place, because the sand, packed tightly under the mold, resists the impression to the point where it becomes literally impossible to sink it to the full depth. When this happens, it is a simple matter to scoop out a depression roughly the size and shape of the mold, leveling the sand to conform as much as possible to the contours of the mold itself, then making the impression.

When the mold has been pressed into position, it is good practice to tap all over the mold sharply before removing it from the sand. This will tend to pack the sand closely around the surface of the mold, compacting it so no loose grains will fall into portions of the cavity before the plaster is poured. If you apply too much pressure in the tapping, however, it will drive the mold down into the sand, enlarging the cavity, so take a moderate amount of care and you will be all right.

KINDS OF CASTING MATERIAL

There are many kinds of plasters that can be used for sand casting. The commonest is plaster of paris. This is fine for all items used indoors, but it will not withstand weathering or outdoor exposure to the elements. Plaster of paris is sold under its own name, or under various brand names. It is the cheapest of the plasters and is readily available. Hardware stores, department stores, paint stores, lumber yards, and building supply houses all handle plaster of paris. It is sold in packages from one pound to one hundred pounds.

Casting stone is another kind of plaster which can be used for exterior work. This is sold by art supply houses, and is a bit more expensive than the common plaster of paris. Casting stone comes in several colors, but the color of the plaster need be of no consequence in our craft, since the entire surface is hidden by the coating of sand anyway. Some brands of casting stone must be treated before they can withstand exterior weather conditions. The treatment consists of adding waterproofing compounds while mixing the plaster. The compounds are sold in building supply houses. Other kinds of casting stone can be used outdoors if the finished casting is sprayed with waterproofing liquids sold for the purpose by the companies making the casting material. You should be able to find one brand or another in stores near you.

One brand of material is Vatican Art Casting Stone, and this is used for indoor pieces as is, or, by giving it several coats of Sculp-metal, is a good exterior product. Sculp-metal is the brand name of the waterproofing compound made by the same company that makes the casting stone. Art and craft companies handle the products or can get them for you in several colors.

Ordinary mortar can also be used for exterior work. There are a few disadvantages to the use of this material, however. The biggest one being that the mortar takes at least an overnight period to set up. Another drawback is that mortar cannot be mixed to easy-flowing consistency as can the casting plasters, but remains a rather thick, pasty mixture which is difficult to cast into delicately detailed cavities. For solid, bold designs, though, it is excellent, and, when finally set up completely, makes strong, practically indestructible castings. Indestructible, that is, to weathering and normal wear. They, like all sand castings, will break if dropped on a hard surface, hit with a hammer, or otherwise physically damaged. Still a third disadvantage to using mortar as a casting material is that, setting as slowly as it does, the time allows the moisture from the mortar to slowly seep down into the sand around the cavity. Ordinarily this would make no difference when using plaster of one kind or another, but in the case of mortar, the water, sand, and cement are all mixed up together. The cement and water are inseparable, and, since water and cement, mixed with sand make mortar, the liquid seeping down into the surrounding sand in the cavity may very well harden the sand into additional mortar, which, when set up, destroys the detail in the casting.

I strongly suggest test pieces made before you make your final casting if you want to use mortar for the casting medium. If you do decide to use it, the mix would be one part of portland cement to three parts of sand, well mixed dry, then add water to make the mixture easy to handle.

PREPARING THE CASTING MEDIUM

The plaster for sand casting should be mixed to the consistency of heavy cream, in order to pour easily, and, more importantly, to be able to dribble into the impression to make the first layer in full detail. I admit that the instructions of mixing to the consistency of heavy cream is somewhat ambiguous. Just how heavy is heavy cream? What might be more practical is to say that the plaster should be mixed to a smooth, heavy liquid, rather than to a thicker paste, so it will pour freely instead of slump into the cavity in the sand. There is, however, a limit to the quantity of water used in a plaster mix. While plaster of paris can be mixed to a quite fluid consistency, if it is made too thin a very poor, weak cast results. Too thin plaster sets to a mealy, spongy state which lacks strength, and never does get completely hard as does a thicker mixture. When well-mixed plaster is completely dry and cured, it has a ring to it when struck—not as clear as pottery, but somewhat on the same order.

Before pouring any of the plaster mixture into your casting box make sure that your piece of hanging wire or twine is at your side and ready to be embedded.

Personally, I prefer wire as being more stable and not subject to deterioration with age. Braided picture wire is fine for the purpose, but this must be treated first, to eliminate the possibility of rusting out at the point of entry into the plaster. The action of plaster on iron wire is rather severe, and very rapid, and a method of protecting the wire from such corrosion must be used *prior* to embedment in the plaster.

The wire is cut to a convenient length, and a loose knot tied in both ends. This knot serves the purpose of anchoring the wire inside the plaster, from which it otherwise may pull out under the strain imposed by the not inconsiderable weight of the plaster casting.

After the knots have been tied, the entire wire should be sprayed with a good coat of clear enamel to prevent corrosion. This is obtainable in spray cans in any paint or hardware store. After spraying one side of the wire, let it dry—which takes only a few minutes—then turn it over and spray the other side.

POURING THE PLASTER

The first coating inside the sand mold should be dribbled from the fingers. Do not be afraid to get your hands into the mixed plaster. As a matter of fact, it is better to perform the entire mixing with the hand rather than with an implement of some kind. This way you can feel that all lumps have been broken up and dissolved, and that the mixture is smooth and homogenous.

Holding the basin or container of plaster over the sand casting box, pick up a small quantity in the fingers of your other hand, dribbling it into the cavity in such a manner as to coat the entire surface of the sand. When this is completed, the rest of the mold may be filled by gently pouring from the container. As you dribble the plaster into the mold, you will note that the water is immediately sucked out of the plaster.

It is important to work right along, without any interruptions, since after the plaster has given up its excess water the remaining plaster poured on top of the drying first layer may not bind well, and the result will be a cast that can separate into different parts. This will not happen if you go right along, dribbling the first coat, then pouring the cast full. You can stop pouring long enough to position hanger wires, and then continue the filling without the danger of the cast separating. It is only if you stop for a long time for one reason or another that you run the risk of layering your casting.

Dribbling the first coating of plaster is even more important when you are making castings containing different ingredients. Small cones, bits of bark, tiny shells, all may float up into the plaster and be lost to sight if dislodged during the filling of the mold. The dribbled first coating will serve to lock these additional decorations in place securely while the cast is being made.

Now, when pouring the second layer, fill the cavity about half full, pouring from a very low height to avoid damaging the impression. Then lay the wire or twine on the plaster, making sure the ends are within the edges of the finished casting, and that the loop for suspension is held up out of the way. Naturally the loop for hanging should be in the center of the top edge of the casting, and attention should be paid to have it in the *exact* center, otherwise the plaque will not hang straight when finished. The wire may be put into position in one of two ways. Either it is projecting up from the top edge of the casting, or it may be placed down from the edge far enough to be hidden by the plaster when in use. If this is the way you desire to have the hanger, you must make some device for holding the wire up out of the way when the remainder of the mold is poured.

Having the wire invisible when the piece is hung is more desirable than having the loop show. It takes a little more time and trouble to hold the wire free, but a stick laid across the casting box should serve perfectly well. The wire is placed over the stick and the looped or knotted ends bent down to rest on the half-filled plaster. Make sure the wire does not float up when the remainder of the plaster is poured.

REMOVING THE CAST FROM THE MOLD

After making the second pour, wait about an hour for the plaster to set completely. Before the cast is removed from the sand, break off all splashes around the edges by pushing down on them to crack them off at the borderline of the cast. Remove the casting very carefully from the sand. Without touching the surface at all, lay the casting across two small sticks or dowels to dry overnight. The edges may then be cleaned up by cutting or scraping them with a knife blade and the excess sand carefully brushed off.

A useful tool for the purpose of removing loose grains of sand is an ordinary rubber ear syringe. It is not used to blow away the grains, but rather, as a vacuum cleaner. Depressing the bulb, then letting the air in as you hold the nozzle at the unwanted sand grains should pick them up without disturbing the remainder of the impression. You must take care not to touch the molded sand with the nozzle, however, or you will create a small hole when the bulb sucks up the grains.

If the casting is made in a box which itself forms the edges of the cast, then cleaning up is not necessary, since the box will provide clean square edges. Certain kinds of plaques are made in this fashion, and others made with the sand impression forming the boundaries of the piece.

As soon as the cast has been lifted from the bed of sand and placed face up in some convenient place to dry out, all the spills and broken off pieces of plaster should be removed from the sand remaining in the casting box. This is easily done with an old tablespoon, and the sand may be sifted from the plaster bits in a coarse strainer. The sand, of course, being used over, and the plaster spills discarded. Your sand casting project is complete and ready for display.

A PICTURE ESSAY

The picture story which follows shows very clearly the various steps in making a sand casting. These steps are identical in every kind of casting, only the details of treatment differing. By this is meant the addition, for example, of objects embedded in the plaster. As pieces utilizing this treatment are described, photographs of these further details will be shown at that point.

Level the sand in the casting box before making the impression, but do not pack the sand down at all.

The mold is pressed straight down into the sand without wiggling it from side to side. This would distort the impression, and enlarge the cavity.

Tapping the mold lightly all over will compact the sand underneath it and make a cleaner impression. However, do not tap so hard that you drive the mold deeper into the sand.

Lift the mold straight up and out of the sand, taking great care not to have the model scrape the sides of the impression. If this does happen, you may have to make the impression over again to get rid of the loose sand knocked down into the cavity.

*The best way to mix the plaster is with your hand. Mix it
into a thick, smooth liquid, working as rapidly as possible
to give yourself more time to make the casting before the
plaster begins to set up.*

Dribble a light coating of plaster over the entire surface of the impression, taking care not to dislodge any sand around the edges. Use your fingers for this purpose.

Now gently pour plaster into the cavity, filling all corners completely, then filling the middle. Before you completely fill the impression, the hanger wire must be set.

Position the hanger wire in the exact center of the casting, or the finished piece will hang crookedly on the wall. If it needs propping up to keep it out of the plaster, a thin stick or dowel laid across the box will support the wire until the plaster has set.

After the casting has set for at least one hour—preferably two hours—the piece may be removed carefully from the sand casting box, and placed on a support to dry.

After drying overnight, the surplus sand is brushed from the surface of the plaster, leaving the embedded coat in place.

Permit the casting to stand undisturbed until it is completely dry before hanging it in place. If hung while still damp, the wall may be stained behind the casting, and the hanger wire may also pull free.

PART

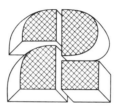

How to
EMBELLISH
and
OFFSET
YOUR
CASTING

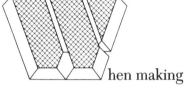hen making additions to a cast, embedding objects to make a design or textured surface other than the sand, remember that the parts of those objects which are buried in the sand are the parts that will be seen when the casting is completed and cleaned up. The parts of the objects visible within the cavity will naturally be buried in the plaster. For this reason, you should pay particular attention to the selection of each object, examining it carefully for the best side to present to view, and taking care that that portion is well embedded in the sand before the plaster is poured. It is a common mistake for a beginner to make a design of stones, shells, bark, or whatever he or she is using, with great pains to

arrange them in the very best pattern, with the best sides showing, and then, after the cast has been removed from the sand to discover to his dismay that the pattern is reversed not only in position, but that all the bad sides of his embedments are the ones presented to the gaze of the viewer.

Another difficulty that occurs in embedding objects is the disturbance of the sand around those objects. Especially if the object is a rough one, such as a bit of bark, or an evergreen cone. This disturbed sand must be cleared away from around the object, and, at the same time, the sand surrounding the embedded part must not be disturbed. It requires a nice touch to scrape or brush away grains of sand on a sand surface without doing damage to that surface. However, with patience and practice you will find it is indeed possible to do just that, and you may take pride in the accomplishment of the completed work.

Bear in mind, too, that minor inequalities on a surface are not too visible when the surface is covered with rough sand. This is not to say that you can just place a mold and let the surface do what it will. It merely means that if there *is* a slight inequality, it does not ruin the piece, because such a spot will be ironed out by the texture of the sand on the surface of the cast.

A WORD OF CAUTION

When you have finished pouring your casting, the container must be washed thoroughly whether you are using plaster of some kind or mortar. You cannot wait too long to clean the vessel or the plaster will harden on the inside, making the container that much harder to clean. And—this is the caution—do not wash the container in a sink, washbasin, bathtub, or toilet. If you do, sooner or later you will plug up the drain, and you can't imagine the cost of having a plaster or cement plug chopped out of your plumbing system. Dump the wash water outside somewhere rather than down a drain. It is far safer. An excellent way to dispose of surplus plaster is to dump it into a plastic kitchen bag where it will harden safely, and then be disposed of without danger to your drains.

The preparation of certain additive components to sand castings requires some thought and practice. Bark, for example, must be trimmed in such a way as to appear as natural as possible around the edges. This means that you cannot, or should not use pieces of bark which have been neatly trimmed to show even smooth borders, because bark never occurs that way in nature. The pieces of bark used for embedment should be cut into the approximate shape, but a bit larger than needed, using a sharp knife, saw, or even chopping with a sharp hatchet. Then all edges should be broken away to produce the final shape and size of each piece. The breaking is best done with pliers, or, if the bark is weak and very brittle, even between the fingers. No attempt should be made to produce exact shapes in bark, since this is a near impossibility. Rather, work with bolder designs, and keep the individual pieces of bark as simple in size and shape as possible.

PRESERVING THE BARK

When using larger pieces of bark, you must take even more precautions against damage and breakage. Bark, after it dries out, is a very fragile material, and yet it lends itself very well to ornamentation, especially in the more modern modes of usage such as we will be discussing here.

Slabs of bark simply must be protected and reinforced in some fashion before they can be used in conjunction with any other kind of material, too.

The best way to reinforce a piece of dry bark is to back it with a rigid material. The thin—$\frac{1}{8}''$

thick—plywood paneling is ideal for this purpose, and the 4′- x 8′-sized sheets are very reasonable in cost. One sheet will last for a great many pieces. Since it is so important to do the reinforcing properly, here are step-by-step instructions as to how to go about it.

First of all, if the bark is extremely dry, you will have trouble pressing it into a flat shape without breaking it into many smaller fragments. For this reason, the bark should be worked very slightly damp. An excellent practice, when collecting the bark, is to put it under a weight to press it flat when you first gather the pieces, and while they are damp and flexible. Lay each piece on a flat, solid surface, and place a board on top of the bark. The board must be large enough to entirely cover the bark. Now put a large stone, brick, or other weight on top of the board and leave the assembly alone for a couple of weeks. If the bark has not thoroughly dried out by that time, leave it a while longer. When all the pieces of bark have been dried, they can be stored flat in a box, stacked one piece on top of another, with several sheets of newspaper or a sheet of corrugated cardboard between each piece of bark. They will keep in this manner for years, provided they are not disturbed.

To reinforce a piece for our work, lay the plywood backing facedown on a work surface, and the bark faceup on the back of the plywood. It is important to make sure you have this sequence right, or the backing will be cut reversed. Draw around the edges of the bark with a soft pencil. Do not attempt to draw every single ripple or indentation in the bark, but just the outline as close to it as you can draw without breaking chips off the edges. Hold the bark firmly against the plywood with one hand flat on top while you draw.

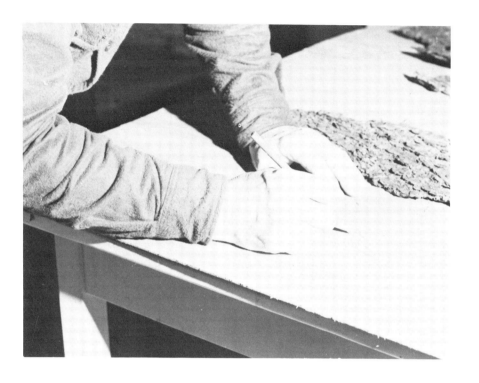

Now remove the bark and draw a second line approximately one-half inch inside the first outline. This is the mark on which you will cut out the plywood.

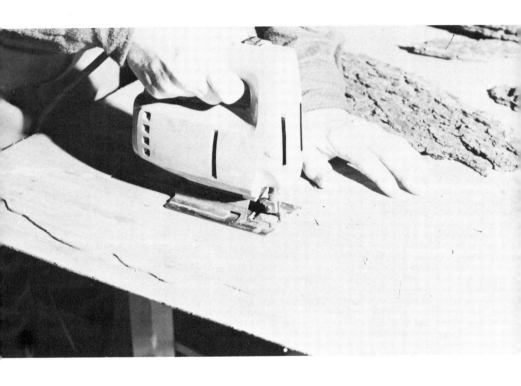

The cutting may be done with any convenient tool. A coping saw, fretsaw, on a power jigsaw, or with a saber saw as shown here.

After the backing piece has been cut from the sheet of plywood, the edges should be darkened. This is easily done with one of the marking bottles, either black or dark brown. This blackening of the edge will effectively conceal the backing board from sight when the piece is finished.

The board must now be fastened to the bark. If you were careful to have the plywood facedown and the bark faceup when drawing the outline, you will now find that the board fits the bark perfectly, leaving a narrow edge all around, and the finished surface of the plywood will be on the outside, giving a finished appearance to the assembly.

Before starting the assembly, you should have everything together that you will need for the operation. The bark, the backing board, a board as large as the piece of bark, for a pressing board, glue, glue brush and clamps. These last may be the spring clamps found in every hardware store, and which require no adjustment other than squeezing them open, slipping them over the work, and releasing the handles.

You should also have a soft yielding pad of some kind to apply pressure to the face of the bark when gluing under the clamps. An ideal material for this purpose is a piece of the cushioned rubber sheeting used under wall-to-wall carpets. Almost any store that sells carpeting also sells the underlayment, and they are practically certain to have some scraps around that they would be happy to give you. At any event, a yard of the material will cost practically

Using a generous quantity of glue—the white glue available everywhere is fine for the purpose—put a good coating on the back of the plywood, position it in place on the back of the bark and slip at least four spring clamps over the edges, clamping the board, pad, bark, and plywood all together. Leave clamped up until the glue sets, then remove the clamps and the piece is finished, ready to be used in our sand casting experiment.

nothing if you have to pay for it. Cut a piece big enough to cover the bark and lay it in place on the face of the bark. Now place a board over the rubber pad, and turn the assembly over.

The bark may be left natural in color, or sprayed with any color you like, or perhaps one of the metallics such as silver or gold would go well with the decor of the room in which you are going to hang it.

An interesting wall ornament may be made by having one section of it—in this case the bark section—standing off the background. A plain slab of sand cast plaster is made to form the backing piece. In the plaster should be imbedded two or three support posts to hold the bark securely.

MAKING AN OFFSET SAND CASTING

The impression for the casting may be made with a plain piece of board cut to the size needed for the bark. At least two or three inches of sand casting should be visible all around the edges of the bark. If the mold is $\frac{3}{4}''$ thick, you will need three pieces of dowel, about $\frac{3}{8}''$ in diameter, and as long as the thickness of the backing slab, plus the distance you want the bark to stand out from the surface of the sand casting. A good distance for this would be about 1″. Whatever distance you decide upon, this dimension should be marked on each piece of dowel as a gauge.

The impression is made by the board mold in the damp sand, then, carefully hold the bark facedown over the impression, but not touching the sand, to locate the spots where the supports can go. The support posts are pushed down into the sand until the mark is reached. The part remaining in view should be the thickness of the plaster which you are going to pour into the mold. Make certain, when embedding the supports, that you get them vertical and true. They should be placed well within the boundaries of the bark, but not so close together that they lose their supporting action. Place them in a triangle, two at one end and one at the other end. Using three supports instead of two affords two great advantages. The first being that the bark is steady on a tripod base, and, even if you do not get the support posts exactly evenly pushed into the sand, the bark will not rock back and forth. The other is that there will be no danger of the bark breaking off the supports as it could if only two supports were used.

Now the plaster is poured into the sand, using the

regular pouring technique as previously described. Dribble the first coat as usual before filling the cavity. Don't forget to embed a hanger wire before the mold is completely poured.

In making offset sand castings, about the only thing you have to watch is to have the sand casting box deep enough to permit the embedment of the standards supporting the offsets. Some of these supports may be quite long, presenting the item quite a distance out from the surface of the sand casting. Naturally, this length must be embedded in the sand before the plaster is poured, and you must have room enough to do this properly. Rarely will you want to hold parts farther away from the sand surface than four or five inches, however, and these dimensions are easily obtained by using a sand casting box made according to the directions given in the first part of the book.

Almost anything can be used for supports in an offset sand casting. When the supports are hidden as in the one just described, then dowels are fine. Often you may want to have the support show as part of the overall design, and then your imagination is the only limit to the number of things you could utilize for the purpose.

Following is a picture summary of this section.

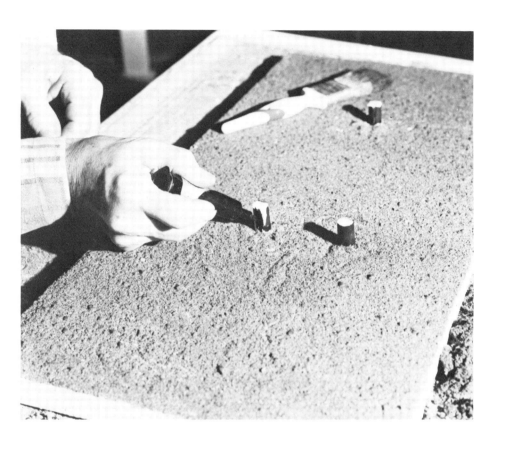

After the plaster has set up and the casting removed from
the sand casting box and cleaned, the dowel supports are
blackened with a marking bottle.

Now the bark is securely glued to the support posts. This is easily accomplished by resting the sand casting firmly on a level base, then placing a mound of glue on the tops of each of the posts.

Now carefully lower the bark into position, centering it before you touch the glue, then lowering it into position without moving it about after the glue is touched. Let the assembly remain undisturbed until the glue has set, and the piece is ready to hang.

Offsetting one of the component parts of a casting in this manner affords a three-dimensional look that is pleasing under certain circumstances. The shadows cast by the top part form a pleasing design in addition to the one obtained by the piece itself.

PART

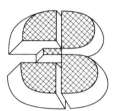

A
GALLERY
of
SAND CASTING
PROJECTS

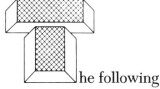he following
portfolio of sand casting projects is offered for your
study. They may supply you with ideas from which
you can develop your own pieces.

Any variation in technique from the regular
instructions given in the first section of this book are
discussed individually.

By frequenting all kinds of secondhand and curio
shops you will find a great number of items that can
be used to embellish a sand casting. Remember that
the only limit to the things you can do is your
imagination. Many persons are very talented in
thinking up designs and creative work. Others must
follow in the lead of these people until they, too,
develop their own ideas. In the beginning, by
copying a few pieces designed by more professional
people, the novice will soon develop his own skills,
and then no longer will he be dependent upon the
ideas of others.

It is an excellent idea, when attacking a new craft,
to follow implicitly the instructions given for one or
more pieces in order to familiarize yourself with the
simple mechanics of the craft. After that you can go
on your own.

LION

This lion's face makes an interesting wall hanging or door ornament. The model used was a piece of ceramics greenware. Old door knockers, mirror, or furniture ornamental finials also can be used to make the sand impression.

EAGLE

Eagles are always popular. In fact, many people collect eagles in any and all forms. The model for this interesting wall ornament came from a ceramics company in the form of greenware. Fired to a bisque it has made many sand castings.

73

ZODIAC

The signs of the Zodiac can be used either singly—as in the case of your own sign—or as a complete set of twelve.

Greenware plaques are available, as well as wood carvings and metal castings. If you are handy with tools, you might even carve out your own. Use bold lines and figures if you do.

FLOWER POT

While the model for this piece was a ceramics ash tray, the sand casting makes an ideal liner for a favored flower in its pot. Use one of the waterproof casting materials, or spray the finished casting with waterproofing compound.

ELEPHANT

PROJECT 5

There are literally dozens of whimsical ceramics molds for use in the child's room. This little elephant makes an interesting wall ornament when cast in colored sand.

O W L

For this piece a ceramics greenware mold supplied the initial shape from which the sand impression was made. Then pieces of dried bark were cut to make the feathers, imbedding these in the sand in an overlapping position. Make sure that the overlap is made so the pieces lie in the natural overlapping sequence when the casting is removed from the sand. Start at the top and place each succeeding feather over the lower end of the preceding one. Just the reverse of shingling.

TOMAHAWK

The crudity of the battle point gives character to this piece, which is adapted from a ceramics greenware mold to make a flat-backed wall ornament. Looks good over a fireplace, too.

PLAQUE

Any kind of plaque with strong, bold designs makes a good article for sand casting. These can be used for wall hangings, foundation tiles, or many other conditions.

A dried lotus pod imbedded in the sand makes an interesting wall plaque.

CHESSMEN

PROJECT 10

*Checkers, or in this case, checker-shaped chessmen make
an eye provoking abstract.*

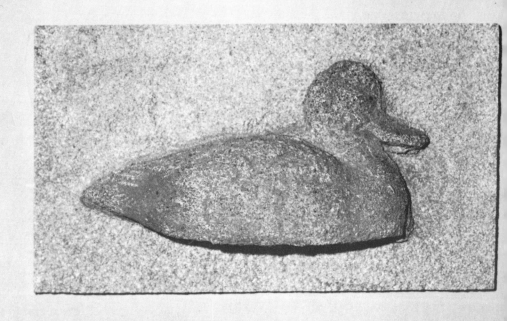

DUCK

In this large plaque the method of making the impression varies slightly from the usual. The sand is raked level, and kept as loose as possible in the box. Now the impression— this one made by a duck decoy—is made in the center of the box. After this cavity is formed, a board about one inch thick and as large as you wish the background to be is very carefully laid on top of the impression. Now damp sand is packed firmly all around the board, building up the sand level with the wood. Allow at least two inches all around the edges for stability for when you pour the plaster. The board is now lifted cautiously out of the sand, leaving the impression of the duck at a lower level than the base. From now on the filling is done as usual. It will take a good amount of plaster to fill the entire cavity, so use a large container for the mixing.

SHELLS

Small shells lend themselves well to nautical arrangements.

SAND PEBBLES

PROJECT 13

Pebbles are easily found on some beaches, smoothly water-worn and just made for arrangement on a wall hanging.

ABSTRACT DESIGN   PROJECT 14

No particular arrangement is followed in abstract designs
like this one. The purpose is to make an eye-focusing
point in the room, and the tiny neat cones of an American
larch make the accent.

*Beach glass gathered on that seashore vacation trip is put
to use here as an ornamental addition.*

BATIK PRINTING DIES   Project 16

Batik printing dies are made by hand, of hard wood, mostly in the Indonesian countries. The designs of some are very pleasing, and the three-dimensional effect when they are embedded by their handles in a wall plaque is interesting.

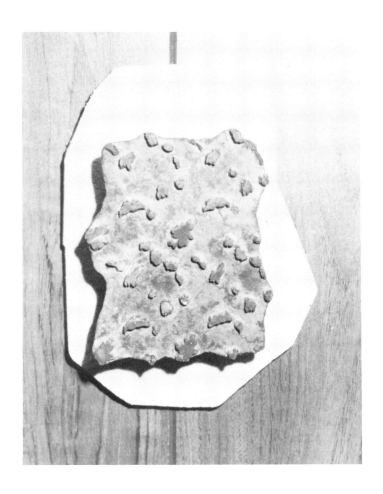

There is no limit to the items that can be used to ornament sand castings. Here we are using an old, used wallpaper printing block. They can be found in many secondhand stores, and now, in gift shops, too.

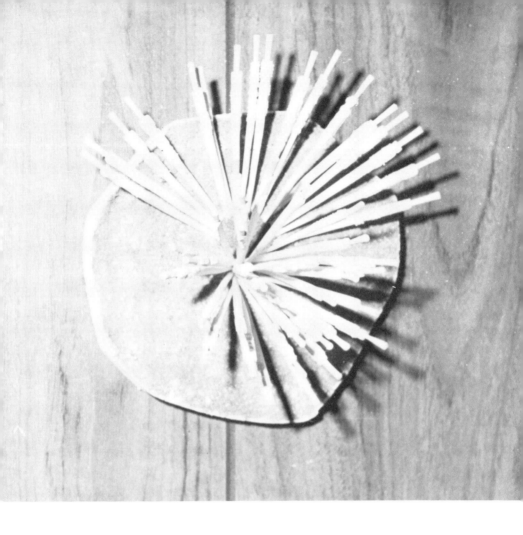

The bunched rods make a bristly ornament in this piece. They are ordinary cocktail picks. The bunches resemble the Lehua blossoms of the tropical islands.

PLANTER

An interesting sand casting planter is made by using a small-handled basket. The handle of this one was cut off to make it more in proportion. The basket should not project too far out from the base. Line the basket with aluminum foil if you intend to plant directly in it, otherwise, the pot containing the plant may be set in the basket without any further protection.

PLANTER

Small planters are always in demand by women who love house plants. A common enameled cup with the handle locked in the plaster base will make an ideal planter for a succulent or small fern. Other plants, too.

CANDLE SCONCE PROJECT 21

A lovely cut glass cordial cup makes the accent point of this casting done in plastic pebbles from a pet store. The pebbles are shiny and smooth, due to their coating of colored plastic, and the plaster of paris seeps through the grains while setting up, making an interesting mottled effect. The glass cup is embedded by its handle, and the piece makes a beautiful wall vase for holding a flower, or it can serve as a candle sconce.

92

MIRROR

*To make this mirror two frames of lattice lumber, ⅜"
thick and 1½" wide are needed. The inside of the first
frame should be the outside dimensions of the frame. The
inside dimensions of the second frame should be one inch
smaller in each direction than the mirror you are going to
use. Level the sand in the box and lay the larger frame on
top, not pressing it down at all. Now bank the sand firmly
all around the outside edges of this frame. Centering the
smaller frame within the larger one, press it down into the
sand to the level of the wood, not disturbing the leveled
sand around the frame. Carefully remove the smaller
frame, leaving a raised center portion in the sand. Now
lay the mirror face down on top of the raised part, with
the overhang even all around. Make your plaster cast as
usual, using the larger frame as the form. If you prefer the
edges of the casting to be sand-covered as well as the
surface, then reduce the size of the larger frame until the
outside dimensions are the size you want the plaque, and,
after packing the banked sand around the outer edges,
carefully remove this frame, too. The sand impression will
now be the form into which to cast the plaster. Don't
forget the hanger wire.*

AZTEC FIGURINE   PROJECT 23

A grotesque Aztec carved lava rock figurine was found in a curio shop. On close inspection it turned out to be plaster, painted and pitted to resemble lava, but that does not preclude its usefulness in a sand casting as a novel and ornamental planter. This time for a family of small sempervivums.

INSECTS

This procession of insects, marching across the bases, can be grouped on a wall for an eye-catcher. The "bugs" were found in a gift shop for less than a dollar each. Made in Hong Kong of nuts, bolts, screws, wire, and sheet metal.

ABSTRACT DESIGN PROJECT 25

Abstract design in colors are made by making a plain impression first, then running the colored gravel in the design on top of the sand. The mottled effect of the colored gravels adds interest to the work.

Often two or more crafts can be combined to make novel projects. Such is the case with sand casting, and candle-making. Sandcast candles are a comparatively new idea, and the following pages will give you an idea or two for making them.

There are several ways to cast wax into sand, each producing a different appearance to the finished article. For a thin coating of sand on the candle, the sand must be quite wet, and for a thick sand covering to the wax the sand should be just damp. The hotter the wax when poured into the sand, the thicker the sand coating will be. You should use a thermometer when melting the wax, and keep the temperature at around 150 degrees for wet sand and a thin coating. The temperature can be raised to around 200 degrees for damp sand and a heavy coating candle.

The molds may be made in almost any fashion. One may also include other ornamentation, such as a small driftwood branch, or, perhaps, small china figures.

Wicks should be of the metal core variety to enable them to stand upright when pouring the wax. They may either be stuck down into the sand, in which case the bottom of the wick must be cut off after the candle is removed from the sand, or they may be placed in metal wick holders, and these pressed lightly into the sand in the bottom of the mold.

A thin wick will burn just the wax around it, slowly creating a well in the candle. Thick wicks will burn the candle more evenly, and also more quickly. If you cannot get a wick thick enough for the candle you wish to make, three lengths of thinner wick may be braided to form one heavier strand.

Candle wax may be purchased in many different stores these days. Almost every hobby shop, department store, craft supply store sells wax and candlemaking accessories. You should add some hardener to the wax as you melt it according to the instructions given with the wax. Colors and perfumes may also be added as desired. One thing to remember is that in sand casting candles the sand covering forms the outside and bottom of the piece instead of the face or top as in regular sand castings in plaster.

PROJECT 26

For this free-form candle, scoop out a hollow in damp sand with the fingers. You need not attempt to make even and smooth walls. The irregularity of the cavity will lend interest to the finished candle. Use a very thick wick or braid three strands of regular wicking, with a metal core. Melt the wax to 150 degrees minimum and 180 degrees maximum. Permit the wax to set up completely before removing the candle from the sand. This may take several hours, so you should let the casting stand overnight.

PROJECT 27

A variation of the free-form candle would be to add a driftwood branch. This is propped up in the sand before the wax is poured. Make sure you place the wick in a location where it will not ignite the branch when the candle is used.

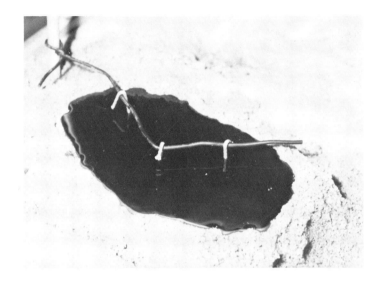

Still another variation is to use more than one wick. When embedding the wax in the sand casting box be sure not to get any sand on the top surface, otherwise you will hinder the burning. Note how the wire is laced through the wicks to allow for easy removal.

A *colorful piece of shale can also be used as a background for the wick in a sandcast candle. These candles can be filled as they burn down and kept useful for a long time. Do not fill the burned out hollows so full as to completely cover the wicks, or they will not light the second time.*

FISH

Diligent sorting through your gathering of pieces will enable you to find sizes and shapes which lend themselves very well to the creation of designs, as in this whimsical fish.

SUNDIAL

The art of science of gnomonics dates back for well over 2000 years. Gnomonics is the art of telling time by the shadow of the sun, and is the principle upon which sundials are made.

Essentially, a sundial is merely a flat plate of any material, having a pointer standing up in the center. This pointer is called the gnomon, and the shadow cast by the sun across the gnomon moves around the plate as the sun moves across the sky. The gnomon can be anything from a rod to a triangular piece of metal. This must be mounted in the center of the plate, and the top edge must slant up from the plate at an angle equal to the latitude in which the sundial is located. The upper tip of the gnomon must point to the north.

SUNDIAL

Another kind of sundial is hung vertically instead of lying flat. A vertical sundial must face south, and the placement of the numerals differs slightly from those of a horizontal instrument. The lower end of the gnomon is set into the plate opposite the numeral 6.

104